The story of wine

MADE IN SOUTH AFRICA

Lynn Barnes

Words that are in bold, like **this**, are explained in the Word help, on the page and at the end of the book.

The *Made in South Africa* series is published by
Awareness Publishing Group (Pty) Ltd.
Copyright © 2019

Awareness Publishing (SA) (Pty) Ltd
www.awareness.co.za
info@awareness.co.za
+27 (0)86 110 1491
www.facebook.com/AwarenessPublishing

All rights reserved. No part of this publication may be reproduced in any form without written permission from the publisher, except by a reviewer.

First edition 2019

The story of wine by Lynn Barnes
ISBN 978-1-77008-994-5

Summary: A simple introduction to wine in South Africa, including a little about its history, different types of wine and how it is made.

Book design: Richard Keenan-Smith and Elizabeth Barnard

Editorial credits: Managing editor: Monique le Riché; Copy editor: Danya Ristić-Schacherl; Picture editors: Anne Laing and Lawrence Frank

Picture credits: Cover © Zoom Team / Shutterstock; cover (background) © AAI FotoStock SA / Alamy / Pete Titmuss; cover (flag) © Kurt / Dreamstime; endpapers © photosiber / Fotolia; p4 © Jacob Lund / Fotolia; p6 © AAI FotoStock SA / Alamy / Art Directors & TRIP; p8 © FreeProd / Fotolia; p10 © estivillml / Fotolia; p11 © Rijksmuseum Amsterdam / Wikipedia; p12 © Jeremy Glyn; p13 © Jne Valokuvaus / Shutterstock; p14 © photosiber / Fotolia; p16 (top far left) © HamsterMan / Shutterstock; p16 (top second from left) © Ninell / Shutterstock; p16 (top second from right) © Dullatum Hanrud / Shutterstock; p16 (top far right) © Shino Iwamura / Shutterstock; p16 (bottom) © AAI FotoStock SA / Alamy / PHILIPPE ROY; p18 © AAI FotoStock SA / Alamy / PHILIPPE ROY; p20 © Brown Reference Group / Elizabeth Barnard & Bianca Keenan-Smith; p22 © Marisa Estivill / Fotolia; p23 © Shchipkova Elena / Shutterstock; p24 © AAI FotoStock SA / Alamy / Chris Fredriksson; p25 © Anna Khomulo / Fotolia; p26 © Jacob Lund / Fotolia; p27 © ulldellebre / iStock; p28 (top) © Anton Chalakov / Fotolia; p28 (bottom) © A.B.G. / Shutterstock; p30 © MrPants / iStock; p32 © Jeremy Glyn; p34 © AAI FotoStock SA / Alamy / Olaf Doering; p36 © Monticello / iStock

1 3 5 7 9 0 8 6 4 2

Contents

South African wines..5
What is wine?...7
Growing grapes..9
The first wine in South Africa..11
Different types of wine...13
Red wine...15
White wine..17
Rosé wine...19
South Africa's winelands..21
Growing the grapes..23
Picking the grapes..25
Squeezing the juice from the grapes..................................27
Making white wine...29
Making red and rosé wine...31
Blending..33
Bottling and labelling...35
Word help...37

A couple enjoying wine with a meal.

South African wines

South Africa is the 9th largest producer of wine in the world.

Wine is made from grapes, which grow well in parts of South Africa. Many people enjoy drinking wine.

Wine made in South Africa is sold to other countries all over the world.

Pictures found inside burial places from 3 000 years ago show that people were already making wine long ago.

What is wine?

Wine is an **alcoholic** drink made from fruit, especially grapes. Fruit contains a lot of sugar and when fruit becomes very **ripe** the sugar turns into alcohol. People discovered this, possibly by accident, thousands of years ago. They liked the taste and started collecting fruit so that they could make their own wine to drink.

> **Word help**
>
> **alcoholic:** containing alcohol
>
> **ripe:** fully grown and ready for eating

A vineyard in Bordeaux, France, which is an area known for good wines.

Growing grapes

Eventually people started growing their own grapes to make wine.

Grapes grow on a plant called a vine. A field full of grape vines is called a vineyard (we say: VIN-yard).

Growing grapes and making wine in modern times first became popular in Europe.

A vineyard in the Constantia valley, Western Cape. Constantia has the oldest vineyards in South Africa.

The first wine in South Africa

Jan van Riebeeck arrived at the Cape in 1652. He saw that the **climate** would be good for growing grapes and he arranged for some plants to be sent from France. These arrived in 1655 and the first vineyards were planted. In 1659 Van Riebeeck made the first wine from the grapes that were grown on these vines. And so the story of wine in South Africa began.

> **Word help**
> **climate:** the kind of weather a place usually has

Jan van Riebeeck.

A waitress carrying three types of wine: white wine, rosé wine and red wine.

Different types of wine

Many types of wine are made in South Africa. Wine can be different colours – red, white or pink. It can also be **still** or **sparkling**. The taste of the wine depends on the type of grapes that are used to make it.

> **Word help**
> **still:** without bubbles
> **sparkling:** with bubbles, fizzy

Sparkling wine has bubbles in it.

Three glasses of red wine showing how the colour can vary from light red to a dark red.

Red wine

Red wine is made from the darker-coloured types of grapes, with purple or black skins. It is the skins of the grapes that give wine the red colour.

Red wine can vary in colour from light red to deep purple or brownish red.

Grapes can be different colours on the outside but their insides are mostly a light colour.

White wine varies in colour from very light to yellow or greenish.

White wine

The flesh inside all grapes is a light colour. So white wine can be made from grapes of any colour, as long as the skins are not used. But white wine is usually made from green or yellow grapes.

The colour of white wine can vary from almost clear, like water, to light yellow or greenish.

White wines also vary in sweetness. A wine that is not sweet is called a dry wine.

The colour of rosé wine depends on how long the grape skins were left in the juice.

Rosé wine

Rosé (we say: ro-ZAY) wine is pink. It can be made from grapes of any colour. It is made by using some red grape skins to give it colour, but not enough to make it a red wine. The longer the skins are kept with the grape juice the darker the colour.

The main wine-making regions are in Western Cape.

South Africa's winelands

There are some vineyards in other parts of the country, but the main wine-making regions are in Western Cape. The area has a good climate for growing grapes, with cool, wet winters and dry summers with lots of sunshine. There are many vineyards and **wineries** and the area is called the Cape Winelands. People come from all over the world to taste the wines made here.

> **Word help**
>
> **wineries:** places that make wine

Grape vines planted in long rows in a vineyard near Wellington in the Cape Winelands.

Growing the grapes

Grape vines are usually planted in long rows with plenty of space in between. The leaves are often held up by wires to let some sunshine get to the grapes, but not enough to burn them. The grapes grow in bunches on the vines.

Bunches of grapes on a grape vine.

Workers picking grapes in a vineyard.

Picking the grapes

The grapes are usually ripe and ready for picking in about February or March. Using machines to pick the grapes can damage them so people sometimes pick the grapes by hand. Heat can also damage the grapes so, if it is very hot, the grapes are sometimes picked at night when it is cooler.

A worker carefully cutting a bunch of grapes off the vine.

Grapes being taken from the fields to a winery.

Squeezing the juice from the grapes

The grapes are taken to the winery and any stems and leaves are removed. This can be done by hand or by a machine. Then the grapes are put into a machine called a press, which squeezes out the juice.

Did you know?

In olden times people used to squeeze the juice out of the grapes by squashing them with their feet.

Stainless steel containers.

Wooden barrels.

Making white wine

When making white wine, the skins of the grapes are taken out of the juice straight away. The juice is then stored in large containers in a cool place and kept until the sugar turns into alcohol. This is called fermentation.

Wineries may store the wine in stainless steel containers or wooden barrels. The wine is often stored in an underground room to keep it cool. This room is called a wine cellar.

A wine maker taking some red wine from a barrel to taste it.

Making red and rosé wine

When making red and rosé wine, the skins of the grapes are not taken out of the juice immediately. They are left in the juice so that some colour from the skins turns the juice red. The longer the skins are in the juice, the redder the wine will be. The grape juice is then also stored and kept to allow fermentation to happen.

Two bottles of different types of red wine. The one on the left is made of merlot grapes and the one on the right is a blend of merlot and cabernet sauvignon grapes.

Blending

There are many different types of grapes and each type produces a particular flavour of wine. Some wines are made using grapes of only one type. Other wines are made by mixing different wines together. This is called blending.

> **Did you know?**
> Wine is named after the type of grapes used to make it. Merlot (we say: mer-low) and cabernet sauvignon (we say: cab-er-nay-saw-vee-nyon) are types of black grapes used to make red wines.

This machine fills bottles with wine. A bottle of wine usually contains 750 millilitres.

Bottling and labelling

Once the wine maker is happy with the taste of the wine, it is put into bottles, covered with a cap or a cork and labelled. Then it is ready to be sent to shops to be sold.

South African wines have won many prizes in world competitions for the best wines.

Wine bottles come in various shapes and sizes.

Word help

alcoholic: containing alcohol

climate: the kind of weather a place usually has

ripe: fully grown and ready for eating

sparkling: with bubbles, fizzy

still: without bubbles

wineries: places that make wine

www.ingramcontent.com/pod-product-compliance
Lightning Source LLC
Chambersburg PA
CBHW051259110526
44589CB00025B/2889